peacock

and other poems

by Valerie Worth
pictures by Natalie Babbitt

Farrar, Straus and Giroux
New York

"Old Hound" first appeared in *Dog Poems*, edited by Myra Cohn Livingston, Holiday House, New York, 1990.

"Lunchbox" and "Ice Cream" first appeared in *Sunflakes*, edited by Lilian Moore, Clarion Books, New York, 1992.

Library of Congress Cataloging-in-Publication Data
Worth, Valerie.
  Peacock and other poems / by Valerie Worth ; pictures by Natalie Babbitt.—
1st ed.
   p. cm.
  ISBN 0-374-35766-8
  1. Children's poetry, American. [1. American poetry.] I. Babbitt, Natalie, ill.
II. Title.

PS3573.O697 P4 2002
811'.54—dc21

2001023828

In memory of Valerie Worth Bahlke
—G. W. B. & N. B.

peacock and other poems

prism

Who'd dream that
A wan little wedge
Of common glass

Could pry from
The proud white sun
These jewels of color!

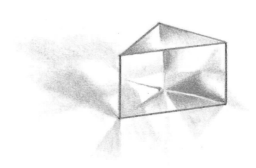

geraniums

The shore
Cottage
That I like
Best has
Cracked steps,
A patched
Screen door,
And two
Concrete urns
Crammed with
Geraniums.

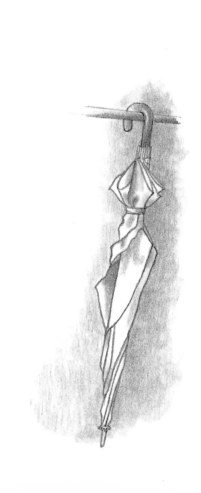

umbrella

Slack wings
Folded, it
Hangs by a
Claw in
The closet,

Sleeping,
Or moping,
Or quietly
Hatching
A plot

To flap out
And escape
On the furious
Sweep of
The storm.

peacock

He fans
Out that
Famous halo,

Turns it
About for
All to see,

Folds it
Down and
Saunters away,

Trailing his
Heavy burden
Of beauty.

(Meanwhile,
His freckled
Brown wife

Rambles around
Him, plain
And free.)

katydid

Bolder than
The cricket,
With its fine
Green suit,
Its long

Sweeping horns,
Its solitary
Singing in
The dark:
Flinging out

Its signature
In a bright
Scratch across
The slate
Of the night.

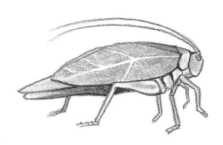

pencil

Plied over
Empty paper,
The shadowy

Tip of
This thin
Gold wand

Conjures up
Anything,
Everything.

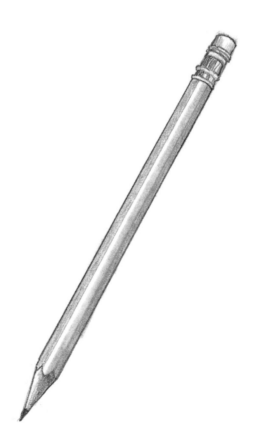

october

Frost a
Presence in
The woods:

A sound
Of footfalls,
One here,

One there,
As the leaves
Step down.

steam engines

They are gone,
All herded into
Scrapyards, the

Grim iron
Locomotives with
Their long boilers,

Their complicated
Plates and domes
And pistons;

But I still
Meet their looming
Ghosts in dreams.

milkweed

The rough
Gray pod
Dries dead,
Splits wide,

And looses
A flight
Of little
Silken souls.

blue jeans

Anonymous
Cloth when
They're new;

Impersonal,
Neat as
A pin,

But slowly
Ripening into
A friendliness,

A homely
Familiar
Skin.

onion

Under its papery
Seal, shell
After gleaming
Shell to the
Inmost pearl:

World within
World, even
While the
Shallow describes
The deep—

So simple,
After all,
As to make
One smile
Or weep.

old hound

When we walk by
The house with
The sagging porch
He shambles forth,
Stout and dowdy on
Wooden-jointed legs,
Raises a faded
Snout, and whispers
Out an echo of
His bygone bellow.

ocean

Listen: its name,
Ocean, held
Like a shell
To the ear,

Echoes its
Moan, its rush,
Its run
To the shore.

panda

Comical puzzle
Of light
And shade,

Masked
Like a
Skull,

Bright grin
Beneath
Black sockets—

Alive and
Joking, fat
Skeleton laughing.

cellar

The dank cement,
The bleak electric
Bulb, the cobwebbed
Windows overhead;

The dust mop
Skulking like a
Sly goblin in
An inky corner.

lunchbox

They always
End up
Fighting—

The soft
Square
Sandwich,

The round
Heavy
Apple.

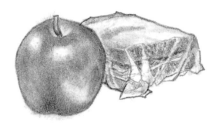

roller coaster

The sluggish
Clattering
Climb, the
Crest, then
Everything
Falls away:

Nothing
Mattering
But the
Wrenching
Track, the
Hurtling car,

The fingers
Clenched
Like death
On the
Slippery
Safety bar.

hammer and nail

Crested steel
Woodpecker,
Knocking and
Knocking so
Hard with its
Obstinate head
That its beak
Has worn
Perfectly flat;

Pitiful
Mannikin,
Sinking away
To his knees,
To his waist,
To his neck,
Until all
You can see
Is his hat.

icicles

When they
Finally fall
And litter
The snow
With splinters
Of clear
Rock candy,

How sad
To discover
That rather
Than sugar
They only
Taste of
The roof.

crayons

Their paper
Torn, their
Snapped sticks

Worn down
To grubby
Stubs, they

Still shed
The colors of
The rainbow.

clouds

Never believe
That clouds
Are mere
Airy vapor:

They are
High terraces
Of marble
And alabaster,

Pillars of
Quartz, alleys
Of pearl
And silver,

To those
Who weigh
Nothing and
Walk there.

hummingbird

In a whir
Of wings he
Floats at the
Flower's door,

Wearing his white
Silk vest,
His glistening
Ruby collar:

And who could
Refuse a sip
Of nectar to
Such a caller?

snake

Startled, the shy
Brown garter snake
Slithers off
Into the weeds,
Meek as a mouse;

But that slim
Glimpse, that
Slender rustling,
Hold the whole
Garden spellbound.

ice cream

Melting, it
Softly fills
The mouth

With something
Like the velvet
Word *vanilla*.

fish

Looking as if
It could still
Swim, looking

As solid as ever
In its orderly
Scales, looking

Up from its tray
Of snow with
A dolorous eye.

wolf

There really isn't
A wolf crouched
Under my bed,

Waiting the chance
To snap at
My naked ankles;

I've looked, and
Never found anything
Worse than dust,

And a silent,
Patient, watchful
Bristling darkness.